Tuning Into God
SMALL GROUP GUIDE

Forty Licks

Steve Idle

Standard
PUBLISHING
Bringing The Word to Life

Cincinnati, Ohio

Published by Standard Publishing, Cincinnati, Ohio
www.standardpub.com

Copyright © 2007 by Standard Publishing. All rights reserved. No part of this book may be reproduced in any form, except for brief quotations in reviews, without the written permission of the publisher.

Printed in the United States of America.

Written by: Steve Idle
Project editors: Michael Mack and Jim Eichenberger
Cover and interior design: Andrew Quach

All Scripture quotations, unless otherwise indicated, are taken from the HOLY BIBLE, NEW INTERNATIONAL VERSION®. NIV®. Copyright © 1973, 1978, 1984 by International Bible Society. Used by permission of Zondervan. All rights reserved.

Scripture quotations marked (NLT) are taken from the Holy Bible, *New Living Translation*, copyright © 1996. Used by permission of Tyndale House Publishers, Inc., Wheaton, Illinois 60189. All rights reserved.

Scripture quotations marked (NASV) are taken from the *New American Standard Bible*. Copyright © 1960, 1962, 1963, 1968, 1971, 1972, 1973, 1975, 1977 by The Lockman Foundation. Used by permission. All rights reserved.

ISBN 978-0-7847-1996-1

14 13 12 11 10 09 08 07   9 8 7 6 5 4 3 2 1

Tuning Into God: ROLLING STONES:

Forty Licks

Table of Contents

Series Introduction 4

Author's Preface 7

Fast Facts about the Rolling Stones 8

1. Satisfaction 9
Finding Contentment • (Philippians 4:4-13)

2. You Can't Always Get What You Want 15
Resolving Conflict • (James 4:1-3)

3. Under My Thumb 21
Improving Relationships • (Ephesians 5:21-32)

4. Let's Spend the Night Together 27
Avoiding Lust • (1 Thessalonians 4:3-8;
1 Corinthians 6:13, 18-20)

5. Sympathy for the Devil 33
Battling Evil • (Ephesians 6:10-18)

6. Paint It Black 39
Overcoming Discouragement • (Ephesians 3:13-21;
Isaiah 40:28-31)

The Rolling Stones on the Web 45

Bible Study Web Sites 46

Icebreakers 47

"Music . . . can name the unnameable and communicate the unknowable." —Leonard Bernstein

"Music is a higher revelation than wisdom or philosophy." —Ludwig Van Beethoven

Introducing . . . Tuning Into God!

"Tune your ears to wisdom, and concentrate on understanding" (Proverbs 2:2, *NLT*).

This discussion guide uses a fresh approach to help draw people, regardless of where they are on their spiritual journeys, into a closer relationship with God.

The **Tuning Into God** series is designed to help you and your group:
- develop a deeper understanding of and relationship with God as you look at his Word from brand new perspectives
- be a creative tool to help you reach out to your friends with his message of grace (for instance, in a "seeker" study in your neighborhood or workplace)

The O'Jays' song title, "I Love Music (Any Kind of Music)" says it well! God created each one of us with a musical "soul"! Apparently, God loves music too. Throughout Scripture, we are directed to sing and play music to him. All of his creation—both in Heaven and on earth—is encouraged to "sing for joy" and "burst into song" (Isaiah 44:23). God is even described as our strength and our song (Exodus 15:2; Psalm 118:14; Isaiah 12:2). Music—any kind of music—has the ability to flow into our souls and move us like nothing else can.

Johann Sebastian Bach once said, "The aim and final end of *all* music should be none other than the glory of God and the refreshment of the soul." Even secular music can accomplish that aim. God uses everything in his creation to accomplish his will, even when those things were never intended by their human authors for his purposes (see Isaiah 46:10, 11; Exodus 9:16; Romans 9:17).

◉ Engaging the Culture

This discussion guide uses popular and spiritually provocative secular songs to engage the culture in which we live. These songs are worldly in nature, so they will, of course, contain worldly words and ideas. Our purpose is not to conform ourselves to these worldly patterns, but to set them next to God's Word to see them for what they are, and then to be transformed by the renewing of our minds (Romans 12:2) as we study and apply Scripture.

Much of secular music is simply a sharing of ideas around some of life's most pressing issues—even around the meaning of life itself. The expression of these ideas through music is much like the Athenians' sharing of the latest ideas in Acts 17. Paul engaged the culture and then interjected God's Word into it. Today, we can also help people who are earnestly seeking to find the "unknown God" they are searching for.

Yes, you will hear some words and ideas you are not used to hearing in a Christian Bible study! But be assured that God's Word deals with these issues and provides the truth to live by.

◉ How to Use This Guide

All songs used in this guide can be found on *Rolling Stones: Forty Licks* or can be downloaded from a digital music Web site. Each week you will be prompted during the discussion to play the featured song, so have everything ready to listen to the song at that time. Lyrics can be found on numerous Web sites, such as the one listed on page 45 of this book.

Use the selected songs as an entertaining way to launch you into an enlightening study of Scripture. Remember that you'll use this guide not so much to discuss the song, but to dive into God's Word to allow it to transform your mind to God's way of living. If you are the group's leader, be sure to facilitate the discussion so as to spend your time wisely studying God's Word. Gently steer off-track discussions back to what Scripture has to say about the topic.

Each session includes:

The Hook: A light, introductory-style icebreaker that leads the group into the study.

Tune-ology: Brief background material and other interesting information about the song and the author.

Instructions to Play the Song and Lesson Introductory Question: The question simply gets your group to look at the selected song for its overall message and meaning.

Scripture Reading and Discussion: Ask someone from the group to read the Scripture passage, and then use the following questions to get the group digging into and talking about the content of the Bible passage. These questions will move the group toward meaning and understanding. While participants on their own may make references to the song, the leader should direct the discussion back to the Bible passage.

The Bridge: A combination of information, a quote, or an interesting fact, along with several questions that tie the Bible passage back to the lyrics of the song. This section also moves the group toward application of the Bible passage.

Tuning In: Application-oriented questions and/or activities that encourage group members to discuss how they will live out the biblical message. This section usually ends with an activity or question that moves group members to formulate an action plan for living out the application during the upcoming week and may include prayer, journaling, additional Bible study, accountability, encouragement, or other practices.

While this discussion guide does not include ideas for worship, prayer, and planning time for outreach and serving, be sure to integrate these important aspects of group life into your meeting.

"Music and rhythm find their way into the secret places of the soul." —Plato

> "Music speaks what cannot be expressed, soothes the mind and gives it rest, heals the heart and makes it whole, flows from heaven to the soul." —Unknown

○ Author's Preface

While all my friends were out buying Beatles albums, I was always drawn more to the Stones. I'm really not sure why. Maybe it was their image as the "bad boys of rock 'n' roll" as opposed to the clean-cut image of John, Paul, George, and Ringo. I think for me it was just the music.

I can still remember the first time I heard the opening guitar riff of "Satisfaction" and the day I bought the 45 single of "Paint It Black" from a Woolworths store in Toledo, Ohio. I have always felt a connection to Mick, Keith, and the band.

For many people today, the music of the Stones reflects the values and feelings of an entire generation and still speaks to younger fans today, nearly forty-five years after their first single.

In this study you will also find yourself confronted with many of the questions and issues that Mick and Keith wrote about in their songs—issues like finding real contentment in life and facing the forces of evil that we all battle every day.

My hope is that you will be encouraged and strengthened by this study. As the title of another hit from the band says, "It's Only Rock 'n' Roll (But I Like It)."

—Steve Idle

Fast Facts about the Rolling Stones

- Formed in 1962, the Rolling Stones are the longest-lived, continuously active group in rock and roll history.

- Keith Richards and Mick Jagger were childhood acquaintances, both attending the Dartford Maypole County Primary School in London.

- Jagger and Richards became reacquainted in college. Jagger was studying at the London School of Economics, and Richards was attending the Sidcup Art School.

- Jagger and Richards joined with mutual friend Dick Taylor to form the band, Little Boy Blue and the Blue Boys.

- The Blue Boys merged with The Ramrods and Blues Inc., which featured Brian Jones and Ian Stewart, and named the band for the Muddy Waters' song "Rollin' Stone."

- After an appearance on *The Ed Sullivan Show* during The Stones' first American tour in 1964, Sullivan vowed never to have them on his program again. He later changed his mind.

- The Rolling Stones' free concert in Hyde Park (London) on July 5, 1969, has been hailed as the British equivalent of Woodstock, drawing over a quarter of a million fans.

- The Rolling Stones were inducted into the Rock and Roll Hall of Fame in 1989.

⊙ Satisfaction

Finding Contentment • Philippians 4:4-13

The Hook

1. Do you remember the old song, "Don't Worry, Be Happy"? Take a moment to critique its view of contentment.

2. When was a time or two in your life when you were the most content? Why?

In 1965 in a motel room in Clearwater, Florida, Keith Richards woke up with the opening guitar riff and the lyric, "I can't get no satisfaction" in his head. With a portable tape player nearby, Richards recorded the riff and went back to sleep. Later that week in the studio, the tape was played, and it consisted of two minutes of "Satisfaction" and forty minutes of Keith snoring.

Versions of the song have been sung by Otis Redding, Devo, "Weird Al" Yankovic (as a polka!), Björk, and Britney Spears, to name a few. "Sesame Street" also did a version called, "(I can't get no) Cooperation."

Play the song, "Satisfaction"
(Disc One, Track 3, on *Rolling Stones: Forty Licks*).

VH1 recently listed "Satisfaction" first among its "Top 100 Rock Songs." *Rolling Stone* magazine has listed it as second only to Bob Dylan's "Like a Rolling Stone." It stands as one of the band's most popular songs and was played by the Stones in the halftime show of Super Bowl XL more than forty years after it was written. Strangely enough, when band members voted on whether or not to release it as a single in 1965, the only two band members to vote against doing so were its authors, Jagger and Richards!

Upon its release, "Satisfaction" added to the band's reputation as the bad boys of rock and roll. When the Stones performed this song on *The Ed Sullivan Show* in 1966, the censors "bleeped" the sexual references in the last verse.

3. Can you remember the first time you ever heard or owned this song?

4. What are some reasons for its musical and lyrical appeal and longevity?

5. Does the song accurately describe the ways people try to find contentment?

Read Philippians 4:4-13.

6. Pay close attention to verses 4-9. What action steps does Paul say must be done in order to fulfill the command in verse 4?

Contrast these steps to the way people usually look for happiness.

7. Consider verse 11. What did Paul imply when he said he had "learned" to be content? How can what we usually consider to be an emotion (happiness, contentment) be learned?

8. What evidence would indicate that someone has not "learned" to be content? Consider the strong statement in verse 13 as your answer.

The Bridge

Mick Jagger has said that when he wrote the lyrics he was commenting on the vast commercialism he saw in America. Notice that the song, while questioning *wrong* ways to find satisfaction, has nothing to offer concerning a *right* way to do so.

For a time the Rolling Stones, like many in the culture of that day, sought to find contentment by escaping the corrupt world rather than confronting it. A common mechanism for doing so was substance abuse. This method of seeking satisfaction led to one of the most tragic chapters in the band's history.

In 1967, Jagger, Richards, and Jones were arrested a number of times for the possession of drugs. After barely escaping long prison sentences, Jagger and Richards appeared to have severely curtailed their drug use. This was not the case for the incredibly talented Brian Jones, however. Ongoing substance abuse caused Jones to become less and less involved with the band, leading to his separation from them on June 8, 1969. Less than a month later, Jones was found dead in his swimming pool. The official police report ruled the incident as "death by misadventure."

9. Review the counsel of Paul in light of the tragedy of Jones and others like him.

   - In what ways does Paul command us to confront the world rather than seek to escape it?

   - Contrast results of seeking contentment in spite of the world with seeking contentment through escapism.

Tuning In

When Paul was writing to the Philippians, there seemed to be little reason for joy. Paul himself was writing from a Roman prison (Philippians 1:13). Some members in the churches he started were using his imprisonment against him in a bid for power (1:17). A verdict in his trial before Caesar was expected any day. A guilty verdict would mean Paul's death and probable persecution for those associated with him (1:20). We also know that the Philippians already faced "the most severe trial" and "extreme poverty" (2 Corinthians 8:2).

Simply having more never seems to bring contentment. The apostle Paul, living in the midst of a poverty-stricken world, addressed a similar human problem that the Stones saw in a culture of excess and materialism.

10. Why do you think it's so hard for most people to experience true contentment in life? List a few of the most common roadblocks to contentment:

11. What are some common roadblocks to contentment?

12. On a scale of 1 to 5, how would you rate the "inner peace quotient" in your life lately? Why?

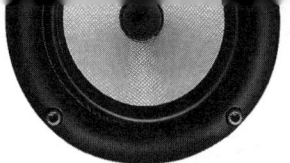

13. One of the things that happens when we follow Christ is that God replaces our old "appetites" for the things of this world (temporal) with new appetites for the things of the Spirit (eternal).

   • Have you noticed your appetite for the things of this world increasing or decreasing in the past six months?

   • Why do you think that is? What do you need to add or subtract from your "menu"?

14. Take a moment and mark two things that you've told yourself you just have to have to be happy.

   ❏ different house   ❏ new job

   ❏ larger salary   ❏ improved spouse

   ❏ better-behaved children   ❏ more free time

   ❏ other_____   ❏ other_____

Through prayer, ask God to release the desire for those things and allow you to experience true contentment.

Session 2

You Can't Always Get What You Want
Resolving Conflict • James 4:1-3

The Hook

1. Tell about a time you heard someone say, "I would kill to have . . ." What did the person want? Despite the fact that everyone would agree that murder is wrong, why do you believe that this exaggerated statement is so widely used?

2. Tell about a time when you wanted something so badly that it had an effect on your attitudes or actions.

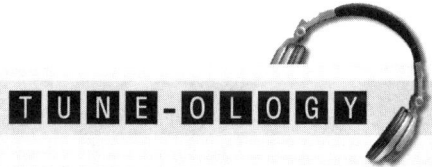

TUNE-OLOGY

"You Can't Always Get What You Want" is one of the few songs on which original Stones drummer Charlie Watts does not play. Unable to master its unusual beat, Watts reportedly walked out on the recording and was replaced by producer Jimmy Miller.

The chorus of children heard at the beginning of the song is the London Bach Choir. Their 60 voices were double-tracked to make it sound like there were even more of them. The choir had second thoughts about their work on this song, however. They tried to distance themselves from it when they discovered that the album on which it appeared was called *Let It Bleed* and contained a song about a serial killer ("Midnight Rambler").

Play the song, "You Can't Always Get What You Want"
(Disc One, Track 6, on *Rolling Stones: Forty Licks*).

As you listen, pay special attention to the arrangement and instrumentation. The use of a children's choir, orchestral touches including the use of a French horn and an organ, and a sing-along chorus sets a distinct mood.

3. What feelings or thoughts does this song evoke in you? What do you remember about the first time you heard this song?

4. In the lyrics themselves we see situations in which people are trying to get what they want in different ways. What words and phrases illustrate some of those situations?

Read James 4:1-3.

5. We all have people in our lives with whom we just don't get along. (Maybe you're sitting next to one right now!) What does James say is the cause of our relational conflict?

6. What is the "battle" James is referring to here? How do these verses relate to this same battle?

   - Romans 7:14-20

   - Galatians 5:16-26

   - 1 John 2:15-17

7. Consider all four of the references we have looked at so far. What words or phrases would you include in a godly prescription for resolving conflict?

The Bridge

Mick Jagger has said that this song is about how hard it is to find real happiness in life and that no matter how good things are, we all still want more. While the lyrics are somewhat vague and metaphorical, many believe that "You Can't Always Get What You Want" is primarily about a woman named Anita Pallenberg. Pallenberg is a part of Stones' lore and has even been labeled as the honorary sixth member of the band.

At the time this song was written, Pallenberg, who had been dating band member Brian Jones, dumped Jones to date Richards. The less than flattering references to the woman in the song reflected the hostility created by the romantic intrigue.

The song also refers to a political demonstration in London as well as a cryptic reference to a meeting in a neighborhood drugstore. One version of the story has Jagger going into the store to get a cherry cola, only to discover that they were out of cherries. A local street person, "Mr. Jimmy" Hutmaker, saw Jagger's disappointment at not being able to get a favorite soft drink and uttered what would become the title of the song.

8. The song has several characters who are in conflict because of issues that differ in relative importance. What biblical advice would you offer to:

   • The treacherous woman who uses deception to get what she wants?

   • The jilted lover who was injured by a broken relationship?

   • The political demonstrator who is angered by political injustice?

   • The customer who did not get the product he wanted?

Tuning In

James was the brother of Jesus and ministered to the church in Jerusalem (Acts 15:13-21). This letter was probably written very early in church history, when the church in Jerusalem consisted of Jews who came to accept Jesus as the long-awaited Messiah. Knowing that the Messiah would be the "Prince of Peace" (Isaiah 9:6), they were probably more than a little discouraged that interpersonal conflict continued in his church!

9. Consider your own view about Christians and conflict.

- When did it become apparent to you that even as a Christian you would still have relational struggles?

- How many of your arguments are caused by the fact that you just want "your own way"?

- In what way do you see a pattern in your life where you consistently blame other people for the conflict between you and never really look at yourself? Explain.

10. What do you think would happen if you went back to that person with whom you have recently argued and said, "You know this bad blood between us? I now realize that part of it is my fault. I just wanted my own way"? (By the way, this probably isn't new information to him or her!)

11. Look again at verse 2. Why does James command us to go to God with all this stuff?

12. What need in your life (security, self-esteem, your identity) have you tried to have fulfilled in other people and never asked God for? (Maybe you've quarreled with them because you're looking for something that only God can supply.)

13. Take some time before you leave and write down one major need in your life that can be fulfilled only by the sufficiency of Christ and not other people. Ask God tonight to supply that for you. Ask at least one group member to join you in that prayer this week.

Session 3

◯ Under My Thumb
Improving Relationships • Ephesians 5:21-32

The Hook

1. Consider one of the following sitcoms. Think of a word or short phrase that describes how it portrays the relationship between husbands and wives: *Leave It to Beaver, I Love Lucy, Happy Days, The Cosby Show, Everybody Loves Raymond.*

2. When you were growing up, what are some factors that shaped your attitudes about the roles of men and women in relationships?

TUNE-OLOGY

"Under My Thumb" first appeared on the album *Aftermath*, but the band never released it as a single. Yet it was one of the most well-known Stones songs of the period. *The Who* did release a cover of the tune, however. Other notable covers were performed by Pentagram in the 70s, an early 80s punk band, Social Distortion, and Canadian rockers, Streetheart. A Spanish version was performed by the Chilean band, Los Miserables.

Musically, the song is noteworthy for the unusual percussion. Brian Jones played the marimbas, doing a variation on the opening riff of the Four Tops' hit, "Same Old Song."

Play the song, "Under My Thumb"
(Disc One, Track 8, on *Rolling Stones: Forty Licks*).

This song was recorded and released in 1966. It deals with roles and relationships between men and women. As you listen, think about how the song would be received were it released for the first time today.

3. Be honest. When you hear this song, how does it make you feel?

4. What line or phrase do you think is the most potentially politically incorrect? Why?

5. Who or what do you think of when you listen to these lyrics?

Read Ephesians 5:21-32.

6. Let's summarize this passage.

    • What is the main message to women, and why?

    • What is the main message to men, and why?

7. Which one of these verses is the "toughest" for you to obey? Explain why.

8. Paul says that a husband is to love his wife "just as Christ loved the church." What words come to your mind to describe that kind of love?

Tuning Into God

The Bridge

"Under my Thumb" is perhaps the most notorious of The Stones' "sexist" songs. Many feminist groups took exception to this song and opposed it because they interpreted the lyrics to be about men dominating women.

9. Reflect again on the lyrics. Which do you think would be the most offensive to feminists? Why?

Reflecting on the track, Jagger claimed it was a parody, not an anti-feminist song at all. Mick Jagger was going out with a model named Chrissie Shrimpton, who reportedly was the eventual inspiration for "Under My Thumb" and other Stones songs. The lyrics are said to phrase the thoughts of a repressed male in a relationship with a pushy woman who dreamed of turning the tables on her.

On the other hand, Keith Richards once said of Jagger, "Mick's attitude towards women is that they are cattle. They are goods. That's his basic attitude."

Many men today seem as confused as Mick Jagger about how to love a woman.

10. Consider the alleged attitudes of both Jagger and Shrimpton.

- How do the instructions in Ephesians 5 help to clear up their confusion about men's and women's relational roles?

- If the apostle Paul were counseling Jagger and Shrimpton, what do you think he would say?

Tuning In

Leader: In a mixed-gender group, consider dividing men and women into two separate subgroups for their last two questions and then pray together.

For men:

11. The apostle Paul lived in a culture that was even more male-dominated than ours today. Yet his teachings often went against the culture. Consider what these verses say about Paul's actions and attitudes about women: Romans 16:1-15 and Galatians 3:26-29

    - How would Paul have been seen as countercultural in his day?

    - How does your view of women compare to the views of non-Christian friends and associates?

12. If you had a good role model to follow as you were growing up, teaching you how a man really loves his wife, please tell the group about him.

    - If not, where did you learn how to love a wife as Christ loved the church?

    - Why is it so difficult for many men to really understand their wives' genuine needs and respond to them in a way that honors God?

    - What steps will you take to do better in this regard?

For women:

13. The apostle Peter also gave instructions on relationships. Quickly skim 1 Peter 3:1-6.

    • Consider the phrases "without words" and "the purity and reverence of your lives" (vv. 1, 2). How have your words to your husband decreased the purity and reverence of your life?

    • Consider the phrase, "do not give way to fear" (v. 6). In what ways has fear kept your from having a healthy relationship?

14. If you had a good role model to follow as you were growing up, teaching you how a woman really loves her husband, please tell the group about her.

    • If not, where did you learn how to be a godly wife?

    • Why is it so difficult for some women to submit to their husbands as to the Lord?

    • What steps will you take this week to improve in this area?

Session 4

◉ Let's Spend the Night Together
Avoiding Lust • 1 Thessalonians 4:3-8; 1 Corinthians 6:13, 18-20

The Hook

1. What are some topics that we often avoid talking about in an informal conversation? Why do you think that taboo exists?

TUNE-OLOGY

While the band was recording this song, two policemen came into the studio. In order to distract them and to dispose of any illegal drugs that were in the studio, the Stones' manager had them record a take with the cops banging their batons for percussion. The batons can be heard about 1:40 into the song.

David Bowie recorded a glam rock cover version of this song for his *Aladdin Sane* album in 1973. In 2003, Sheraton hotels used "Let's Spend the Night Together" as the slogan for their ad campaign. The song was used in the commercials but performed by a California band called Convoy.

Play the song, "Let's Spend the Night Together"
(Disc One, Track 20, on *Rolling Stones: Forty Licks*).

2. As you listen to the song, consider the following:

- What are some words or phrases that might have been considered taboo when this song was first released?

- What was your parents' (or grandparents') reaction to this song? (Or what do you *think* your parents' or grandparents' reaction might have been?)

- Do you think this song would seem as "scandalous" if it were released for the first time today? Why or why not?

Read 1 Thessalonians 4:3-8 and 1 Corinthians 6:13, 18-20.

3. How would you paraphrase the following words and phrases from 1 Thessalonians 4:3, 4?

   - be sanctified

   - avoid sexual immorality

   - learn to control his own body (see footnote in *NIV*)

   - holy and honorable

4. Compare 1 Thessalonians 4:7, 8 to 1 Corinthians 6:13.

   - Note the inclusion of quotation marks in 1 Corinthians 6:13 (also in verse 12). What does this indicate?

   - What do both of these passages say about the source of sexual morality? How does the biblical view vary from the popular view?

5. Popular thinking is that sexual behavior is personal and victimless. What does each of these verses say about that thought? Who are the victims, and how do you think they are victimized?

   - 1 Thessalonians 4:6

   - 1 Corinthians 6:18

   - 1 Corinthians 6:19, 20

The Bridge

The Rolling Stones were basically a blues band that became a rock and roll band. One characteristic of the blues that carried over to their music is dealing frankly with sexuality. This song is a prime example.

In one of the more famous (or infamous) musical television moments, The Stones performed this song on *The Ed Sullivan Show*. Sullivan made them sing "Let's spend *some time* together" in place of the original words. (Mick Jagger sang as ordered, but rolled his eyes in displeasure every time he sang the "new" lyrics.) Many radio stations refused to play the single, preferring to play its B side, "Ruby Tuesday." When it *was* played, the word *night* was often "bleeped" out.

6. Some have labeled Christians as being "anti-sex," arguing that openly discussing sexuality is something positive. (In the 60's it was referred to as being *uptight*; today it is called being *repressed*.)

    - If Paul could have read the lyrics of this and other Stones' songs, do you believe that any objection of his would have been because they were about sexuality, or do you believe he would object for other reasons? Explain.

    - What do you find most intriguing about God's plan for sex? Why do you think unbelievers fail to understand this?

In 1967 the late Stones guitarist Brian Jones said, "Young people are measuring opinion with new yardsticks, and it must mean greater individual freedom of expression. Pop music will have its part to play in all of this."

7. Based on the Scripture texts we have studied, summarize how you think Paul would have reacted to that statement.

Tuning In

Leader: Use your own wisdom and discretion as necessary (knowing the members of your group) as you lead the rest of this potentially sensitive (and yet important) discussion. In a mixed-gender group, consider dividing men and women into two separate subgroups.

8. Take a moment to review our Scripture texts and personally react to them.

    - What emotions did you experience as you read each passage?

    - What previous relationships came to mind?

    - How did you feel about those relationships as you revisited that particular period of your life?

Paul was writing to churches in a culture that was every bit as sexually charged as our own. The patron goddess of Corinth was Aphrodite, the goddess of love. Pagan worship to Aphrodite actually included temple prostitution! Sexual issues such as homosexuality, abortion, and pornography are not of recent vintage, but were very common in the day these words were written.

9. Considering this, how realistic is Paul's advice?

    - What steps should we take when the Bible's definition of sexual immorality is considered normal behavior in society?

    - How is it possible, even for someone with a "sexual history," to still "honor God" with his or her body?

God has been called the "God of the Second Chance." Maybe as you've studied this topic you have experienced guilt, shame, and a sense of personal failure in this area of your life.

There is hope. The battle for sexual purity is just that—a battle. But it can be won. God has already given each of us the resources we need. (Look again at the last phrase in 1 Thessalonians 4:8.) Now it's up to you.

10. On a scale of 1 to 10 (1 being low and 10 high), how would you rate your own level of sexual purity in your:

- thought life?

- words?

- actions?

11. What practical steps do you need to take today to help ensure that you "live a holy life"?

- Have you made a personal commitment of your life to sexual purity?

- Do you need to set some sexual boundaries with your boyfriend, girlfriend, fiancé, or someone else?

- Who in your life can you ask to help hold you accountable?

Session 5

◉ Sympathy for the Devil
Battling Evil • Ephesians 6:10-18

The Hook

1. If Satan gave awards, speculate as to his nominees for the title, "The most evil person in . . ."
   - the business world
   - U.S. politics
   - world politics
   - the entertainment world
   - your personal life

2. When you were in elementary school, what was your image of the devil? How about in high school or college? Has your image of the devil changed now that you're an adult? If so, how?

TUNE-OLOGY

The inspiration for the lyrics allegedly comes from *The Master and Margarita*, a Russian novel. British singer Marianne Faithfull, Mick Jagger's girlfriend at the time, was well-educated and often exposed Jagger to new ideas. In the book, the devil is portrayed as a sophisticated socialite. Some have also seen comparisons between the content of the song and "The Devil and Daniel Webster," a short story by Stephen Vincent Benét.

"Sympathy" has been recorded by Guns 'n' Roses, U2, Blood, Sweat & Tears, Natalie Merchant, Jane's Addiction, the Hampton String Quartet, and, believe it or not, the London Symphony Orchestra.

Play the song, "Sympathy for the Devil"
(Disc One, Track 11, on *Rolling Stones: Forty Licks*).

As you listen to the song, pay attention to both lyrics and the feelings generated by the music itself.

3. What lines or phrases jump out to you? Note lines that refer to:

- biblical history

- the Russian revolution

- World War II

- the Hundred Years War

- political assassination

- societal corruption

In 2006, this song was included in *The National Review* magazine's list of the 50 most conservative rock lyrics. They claimed that this is an anti-Communist, conservative song and that the devil being referred to is Communist Russia. Jagger himself claims this song is about the dark side of man, not a celebration of Satanism.

4. Do you think this song is more about the evil of the devil or the evil deeds of human beings? Defend your answer.

Read Ephesians 6:10-18.

5. Many Christians have mistakenly thought that knowing God ought to make their lives easier. Maybe you have thought that way. Paul is teaching us here that the Christian life is war.

   • Is it surprising to you that part of God's plan for your life is that you actually do battle with the evil one? Why or why not?

   • Compare Ephesians 6:12 to 1 Peter 5:8. How are they saying the same things in dfferent ways? What word(s) tell us that our enemy is not easily defeated?

   • The word Paul uses four times here for "stand" literally means to "hold a critical position while under attack." Describe what that means in everyday terms.

6. List the elements of the armor of God listed in Ephesians 6:14-17. How would a Christian use each one?

The Bridge

Although the Stones were often accused of being interested in Satanism, that charge was regularly denied. Yet the reality of evil was unmistakably present in one of the darkest incidents in the band's history.

In 1969, shortly after the Woodstock festival, the Stones staged a free concert at the unused Altamont Speedway outside of San Francisco. The band hired the local chapter of the Hell's Angels to be in charge of security for the concert. (This was not an original idea. The Grateful Dead had used the motorcycle gang in that capacity many times.) The Hell's Angel's, under the influence of large amounts of free beer given to them as partial payment for their services, came into conflict with the 300,000 fans in attendance. During this song, the battle grew more heated, and while the band performed the next tune ("Under My Thumb"), the gang stabbed and beat Meredith Hunter, a young African-American man, to death for allegedly threatening them with a firearm.

Due to public outcry, the Rolling Stones did not perform "Sympathy for the Devil" for 7 years after the incident. In the hit pop tune "American Pie," Don McLean referred to this tragedy as delighting Satan and contributing to the death of popular music.

7. Paul talks about "the devil's schemes." Do you think the Altamont Festival was one of those schemes? To what extent do you believe the devil was involved in this tragedy?

In a 2002 interview, Keith Richards said, "'Sympathy' is quite an uplifting song. It's just a matter of looking the devil in the face. He's there all the time. . . . You might as well accept the fact that evil is there and deal with it any way you can. 'Sympathy for the Devil' is a song that says, 'Don't forget him. If you confront him, then he's out of a job.'"

8. Would you agree with Keith's assessment that "if you confront him (the devil), then he's out of a job"? Why or why not?

Tuning In

9. Try to place each piece of the armor of God into one of these categories:

   - personal characteristics that protect us from attack—

   - equipment that cannot be destroyed or withstood by Satan—

   - opportunities to unite with other believers for strength—

10. Describe how a believer could use specific pieces of the armor of God in each of these situations:

    - A congregation in a small town has bounced checks to its creditors more than once. That congregation is not growing.

    - A spiteful coworker falsely accuses a believer of embezzling company funds.

    - A Christian is afraid of ministering to AIDS patients.

    - A believer feels unable to answer the questions of an unbelieving friend.

    - A Christian feels like he or she is standing alone in a trial.

11. Which elements of the armor of God are present in your life right now? Which are missing? Out of the options below, pick one, and tell of a time when:

   • you have gotten "tripped up" because you were dishonest.

   • your reputation for righteousness shielded you from the painful consequences of an ugly rumor aimed at you.

   • you just didn't feel like sharing your faith.

   • the presence of other believers made you stronger than you could have been alone.

   • doubts about your salvation made you fearful of death.

   • a Bible verse helped you ward off temptation.

12. No matter how strong our convictions or how solid our biblical understanding may be, we will never be victorious in this battle without putting on the armor of God. Write out a plan for how you will begin using the weapons God has provided for you.

Step one—

Step two—

Step three—

Step four—

Session 6

◯ Paint It Black

Overcoming Discouragement • Ephesians 3:13-21; Isaiah 40:28-31

The Hook

1. The leader should bring a box of crayons to this session. As the study begins, take one crayon out of the box and be prepared to:

   - cite phrases in which the word for that color is used and what it means (ex: "tickled pink" or "red hot fury").

   - list feelings associated with that color.

   - tell about a time when your mood could be described by that color.

"Paint It Black" was released on the album *Aftermath* in 1966, the same time the Beatles released *Revolver* and Bob Dylan released *Blonde on Blonde*. In 2004 it was ranked #174 on *Rolling Stone's* list of the 500 Greatest Songs of All Time. (The Stones had 14 songs on the list, second only to the Beatles' 23.) Legend has it that John Lennon called "Paint it Black" the greatest composition of the twentieth century.

"Paint It Black" has been covered by U2, Deep Purple, Vanessa Carlton, Judas Priest, Rush, Johnny Lang, among others. The song shared its name with a compilation of Stones covers by everyone from Linda Ronstadt to the Ramones.

Tuning Into God

Play the song, "Paint it Black"
(Disc One, Track 17, on *Rolling Stones: Forty Licks*).

Jagger and Richards wrote "Paint It Black." They originally thought of it as being a slow soul song from the viewpoint of a person who is depressed. That person wanted everything to turn black to match his mood. As the song developed, many other musical elements were added. As you listen, see if you can pinpoint strains of rock, R&B, music of the Middle East, and music from the Far East. Note how each contributes to the mood.

2. This song appears to be about a lover who has died. What words and phrases might lead you to that conclusion?

3. What other colors did you hear mentioned in the song? How does each one differ from the blackness the singer feels?

4. Note that the singer expects his blackness to cover up the brightness that others feel. Is that how darkness and light *really* work? Does darkness blot out light, or does light dispel darkness? What does that say about the perspective of a depressed person?

Read Ephesians 3:13-21 and Isaiah 40:27-31.

5. Notice Ephesians 3:13. The *New International Version* uses the words "not to be discouraged," the *King James Version* reads "faint not," and the *New American Standard Bible* uses the phrase "not to lose heart."

   • What do those phrases mean? Which communicates more clearly to you? Why?

   • What is the primary cause of the Ephesians' discouragement according to that verse? Why might that situation bring discouragement?

6. What was the source of discouragement for the people of Israel in Isaiah 40:27? From what you know of the Jews and their periods of exile described in the Old Testament, explain why they may have felt the way they did.

7. Both Paul and Isaiah write a prescription for discouragement. Rephrase each of the following verses as if a doctor were giving orders to a depressed patient:

   • Isaiah 40:28, 29

   • Isaiah 40:30, 31

   • Ephesians 3:14-17a

   • Ephesians 3:17b-19

Tuning Into God

The Bridge

The person Jagger sings about in this song, the Jews in exile, and the believers in the church of Ephesus all seem to be facing the same issue in life. They had all lost heart and felt like giving up because there seemed to be no way out of this darkness.

Other groups wrote sad songs. The Stones wallowed in despair. Other groups wrote of world problems while giving hope of better days. The Stones pointed out the darkest aspects of life without offering solutions.

While other bands were singing lighthearted love ballads and cheery pop anthems, Jagger and Richards wrote of drug-addicted parents ("Mother's Little Helper"), violent anti-war protests ("Street Fighting Man"), and even the infamous serial killer and rapist Albert "The Boston Strangler" DeSalvo ("Midnight Rambler"). Their underlying assumptions seemed to differ greatly from most who were making music at that time.

8. Consider the prescription for discouragement that you discussed from Paul and Isaiah. Take each of those points and write a word of advice to the singer of this song who is mourning the death of his lover:

- Isaiah 40:28, 29

- Isaiah 40:30, 31

- Ephesians 3:14-17a

- Ephesians 3:17b-19

How would these points also apply to the other dark themes of Stones' songs?

Tuning In

We must understand that the Bible is in no way divorced from the real world. Jews in captivity saw the bloody destruction of their homeland, desecration of everything they held sacred, and inhuman violence from some of the most ruthless nations that have existed.

Christians in Ephesus knew of the injustice of Paul's imprisonment. They had heard rumors about the insanity and grotesque immorality of Nero, who ruled their empire. They lived each day in a culture dominated by paganism and immorality. They needed real answers, not trite truisms.

9. What are some of the sources of discouragement in your life right now? What causes you to think that the world is beyond hope? Consider:

   - situations in your personal life that sadden you.

   - changes you see in our country that cause you to lose hope.

   - world problems that seem to be out of control.

10. What do the verses we have studied teach us about the nature and power of God?

11. Notice the phrase, "that Christ may dwell in your hearts" (Ephesians 3:17). The word *dwell* literally means to settle down, to be at home. How does your life reflect this reality?

12. By definition a Christian is one in whom Christ resides as Savior. What changes do you need to make so that he is more welcome and in control?

The Rolling Stones on the Web

Official Web Sites
Band Web site
http://www.rollingstones.com/

Mick Jagger's Web Site
http://www.mickjagger.com/

Keith Richard's Web Site
http://www.keithrichards.com/

Fan Sites
Rolling Stones fan club of Scandinavia, UK, and USA
http://www.stonesplanet.com/

It's Only Rock and Roll—Rolling Stones fan club of Europe
http://www.iorr.org/

Lyrics
Lyrics on the official Web site
http://www.rollingstones.com/discog/index.php?v=&a=1&id=154

Purchasing *Forty Licks*
CD
http://www.amazon.com/Forty-Licks-Rolling-Stones/dp/B000061R69

Download
http://greatmp3download.org/rolling_stones_11661.shtml

Rolling Stones Memorabilia
http://www.irocknroll.com/RollingStones.html

Rolling Stones Ringtones
http://www.moviso.com/search.jsp?artist=The+Rolling+Stones

Sites listing for informational purposes only. Appearance on the list does not constitute an endorsement by Standard Publishing.

Bible Study Web Sites

Bible Text
Search the Bible in over 50 versions and 35 languages
http://www.biblegateway.com/

Online concordance and other handy tools
http://www.blueletterbible.org/

Classic Commentaries
Search more than a dozen commentaries by chapter of the Bible
http://eword.gospelcom.net/comments/

Bible Dictionary
Look up important Bible words and phrases with a simple index
http://bibletools.org/index.cfm/fuseaction/Def.default

Lexicons
Do word studies from the original Hebrew or Greek
http://www.studylight.org/lex/

Bible Study Tools
A variety of tools are found here
http://bible.crosswalk.com/

http://bible.oneplace.com/

Audio Bible
Listen to the Bible in MP3 format
http://heargoodnews.org/Bible/

Cyber Hymnal
Coordinate classic hymns to any study with these searchable indices
http://www.cyberhymnal.org/

Sites listing for informational purposes only. Appearance on the list does not constitute an endorsement by Standard Publishing.

Icebreakers

One of the purposes of a small group Bible study is to get to know one another better. On occasion, you may wish to start a session with one of these games that helps build community in a fun way.

Clusters
At the leader's signal, members need to cluster themselves together according to each of these criteria:
- favorite color
- season of the year in which you were born
- number of siblings
- state in which you were born

The leader will keep the game moving. As soon as one set of clusters is made, he or she will give another criterion to rearrange the group.

I Have Never
The leader should give each group member the same number of "markers" (coins, poker chips, pieces of wrapped candy) as the number of people in the group. Each member, in turn, should make a true statement about himself or herself beginning with the phrase, "I have never." Statements should be about an activity that the member has *not* done, but believes that many others in the group *have* done. For example:
- I have never been to Florida.
- I have never eaten lobster.
- I have never owned a new car.

Each member who *has* done what the speaker has not must give the speaker a marker. Play progresses until all members have had a turn.

Poetic Intros
Each group member is given a few minutes to come up with an introduction of himself or herself that employs a common poetic element. Common examples would include:
- alliteration (Golfing Glenda, Numbers Nick)
- rhyme (Slim Kim, Silly Billy)
- metaphor (Sparks Lewis, Carla the Swan).

Ask members to explain their intros.

Help! I'm a Small Group Leader!

Small Group Help Guides are ideal for any leader who is looking for practical tips to help them begin and lead a small group.

Let's Get Started!
03015 • 9780784720738

Now That's a Good Question!
03038 • 9780784720745

Why Didn't You Warn Me?
03042 • 9780784720752

I'm a Leader . . . Now What?
03050 • 9780784720769

To purchase visit your local Christian bookstore or find it online at www.standardpub.com.

Standard®
PUBLISHING
Bringing The Word to Life